It'll be OKAY, and you will be too.

DR. JEREMY GOLDBERG

THOUGHT CATALOG Books

ISBN 978-0-692-62472-2

10 9 8 7 6 5 4 3 2 1

Why are we not fighting fire with water?
Compassion will not make us lazy.

—*Buddy Wakefield*

THE STORY SO FAR

Hi, I'm Jeremy, and I'm trying to start a kindness revolution in my spare time. It's called Long Distance Love Bombs and I'll tell you all about it, but first I'm going to ask you a question, and then I'm going to tell you a story.

The question is this: "What if kindness was cool?"

And the story?

The story is one I'll never forget. The story starts in an airport.

Years ago, I was standing at the gate, waiting for my flight to board, and I looked over and I saw a woman sitting by herself, talking on the phone, crying loudly and alone. After a minute or two, she put down her phone and just sat there, silently sobbing.

I felt terrible.

After watching her for a few moments, I realized I had to do something. I had to help but I didn't know this lady or what she was going through. She was a stranger. What could I do?

I reached into my wallet and pulled out a card. On the back of it, I wrote, "It'll be okay, and you will be too."

I walked over, looked her in the eyes, and gave her the card. I put my hand on her shoulder for just a second and then I smiled, I turned away, and I walked off. I boarded my flight and I never looked back.

I felt like in that moment we had a connection, and her life was a little bit better as a result of that small action. I felt there was power in that interaction, and I realized there was honor in helping someone get through the day. I don't know what happened next and I don't know what her reaction was, but the whole experience shook me up and I thought about it a lot during my flight.

Why, in an airport filled with people, did nobody else step forward to help this lady? Why was it okay for her to sit and cry by herself, surrounded by a crowd of people staring at telephone screens and magazines? Why, in our society, is indifference so innocent and apathy so acceptable?

I sat on the plane and wondered if this is the best we can do, and I decided that it's not. I decided that it can't be. But what's the alternative? How could we change it? Where do we begin?

I started daydreaming. I pictured the same scenario with the same lady in the same airport crying the same tears, but in my version of reality, I imagined her being bombarded with support. I imagined an old man shuffling over to give her a hug. I pictured a group of teenagers stopping by to ask if they could sing her a song. I saw a couple on their honeymoon walk over and whisper, "You're not alone here."

I feel like that world is possible.

I sat on the plane and started thinking about how to change things. I imagined a world where every time someone was sad, lonely, depressed or in doubt, they knew help was hiding in the heart of everyone around them. I pictured a world where kindness was cool and compassion was popular, a world where we looked after one another and helped each other out, a world where consoling a stranger was not the exception, it was expected. I sat and tried to envision a world like that, a world where instead of posting photos of ourselves online, social media was populated by images of us being generous, kind, and supportive.

What if we were obsessed with giving selflessly, not taking selfies? What kind of world would that be, and how do we get there?

I sat on that plane that day and decided I was going to try to make a difference. I decided I was going to make the world better than it was yesterday and I decided I was going to start trying to make kindness cool. I decided I was going to change the world. There was, however, one little problem: I had no idea what the hell I was doing. I didn't know where to start and I didn't know how to do it. But I had passion, and everything good starts with passion.

I sat and started thinking about what this kindness revolution might look like, and I decided it would be the same as any other revolution. It would start with an idea, and ideas are just words, so I thought I may as well start there, with words.

So, I started writing, and I started sharing, and I started small. Using my airport encounter as inspiration, I began leaving cards in public places, dropping my little long distance love bombs all over the place.

I left notes around town, small encouraging insights, bits of inspiration. I left these cards on bus seats, in stores and restaurants, under windshield wipers...

I liked the idea of surprise, an unexpected epiphany that in our crazy world, a stranger could stumble on a bit of connection, a bit of hope, something helpful. I liked the idea that I could do something to change the world, and I could carry it around with me, I could do it anonymously, easily, cheaply, and freely, anywhere at any time. I liked the idea of leaving a bit of light for others to find.

I hope you do the same.

—Jeremy Goldberg

THE NEXT CHAPTER

You often hear the adage "practice what you preach." For Jeremy Goldberg, the practice was everything. Not only that, but it came from such a genuine place, at the smallest moment. A calling in his heart. A vocation to be cognizant, compassionate, kind. To treat strangers with the same care and concern as we would our friends. To be open to the likeness and otherness of our fellow men, to hold space for them both. To be generous and gentle. Jeremy's work reminds us that it's not enough to be human. If we are going to live our best lives, then we must strive to be good humans. Good to ourselves. And more importantly, good to others.

This book is a collection of Jeremy's notes, poems, letters, and prose. They come chock full of affirmation, positivity, and pep—exactly what you need to put the life back into your step. Whether you're hurting or healing or somewhere in between, there is something in here for you.

But that's not where the story ends.

You can take what you need from these pages. Maybe you leave it by your bed, read and reread it over and again. Or maybe it makes a home on your shelf, collecting dust with all the rest. You can treat this book like any other in your collection. You can, but you won't.

Because you're not that kind of person, are you?

No, there's something different about you. And there's something different about this book. It's not enough to keep these little love bombs to yourself. You want to share them with as many people as you can.

You want to join the movement.

And that's exactly why this book has been designed with you in mind. You, the reader, the changer of the world. You, the proponent of kindness. The ambassador. The practitioner.

So, go ahead. Read your perfectly bound book. Engage in the ideas and meditations. But when you're done, feel free to tear along the dotted lines and pass the kindness on. Put one in a frame. Fold up a poem for your lover to find. Mail one to an old friend. Leave another on a mentor's desk. Keep a couple in your wallet, and carry them with you as part of your love arsenal.

That way, the next time you see a woman silently crying in a sea of strangers, you'll know exactly what to do.

—*Amanda Torroni*

In case you haven't noticed,
I'm turning over a new leaf,
except that my leaf is a forest,
and I'm not turning it over,
I'm burning it down.

IT'LL BE OKAY, AND YOU WILL BE TOO.
DR. JEREMY GOLDBERG

One wing out of my
cocoon and I don't know
where I'm going,
but I'll be soaring soon.

IT'LL BE OKAY, AND YOU WILL BE TOO.
DR. JEREMY GOLDBERG

At the heart of hard is hope,
and that's what life's about—
hope the struggle is worth the fight,
hope to share joy with those we love,
hope things will work out,
and when all is said and done,
when they rest our darkened sparks
in the glowing grounds of tomorrow,
we hope we can rest peacefully
in the hard-earned, hard-fought truth
that in spite of everything life threw at us,
despite the nothing and the nonsense,
the hardships and the horrors,
we were enough,
our lives were enough.

IT'LL BE OKAY, AND YOU WILL BE TOO.
DR. JEREMY GOLDBERG

Life gets better.
It really does,
always will,
simply must.

IT'LL BE OKAY, AND YOU WILL BE TOO.

DR. JEREMY GOLDBERG

May you wake up and be yourself all damn day,
and may you not give a fuck what your critics may say,
or what your friends might think,
or what your loved ones believe.
Your voice is what matters,
the quiet, whispered, knowing breath
that won't ever shout but still always says,
"We survived this before and we'll do it again."

IT'LL BE OKAY, AND YOU WILL BE TOO.

DR. JEREMY GOLDBERG

Just because something glows doesn't mean it's light.

An explosion is bright, but it won't grow a rose.

IT'LL BE OKAY, AND YOU WILL BE TOO.

DR. JEREMY GOLDBERG

Hurt is just another color shade to paint the portrait of hope on the work-in-progress canvas of your heart.

IT'LL BE OKAY, AND YOU WILL BE TOO.

DR. JEREMY GOLDBERG

Go ahead
and take a risk
and make the switch
and choose to live
and dare to dream
and try to think
of all the things
that you could be
if you could see
that we become
what we believe
when we repeat
the truth we need.

IT'LL BE OKAY, AND YOU WILL BE TOO.

DR. JEREMY GOLDBERG

Sometimes our light
takes a nap to recharge.
It's not always pretty,
but that's all the dark is.

IT'LL BE OKAY, AND YOU WILL BE TOO.
DR. JEREMY GOLDBERG

It didn't work out,
but that doesn't mean it won't.

IT'LL BE OKAY, AND YOU WILL BE TOO.

DR. JEREMY GOLDBERG

Stand proud,
for you are a peacock
amongst the penguins.

Soar free,
for you are a flamingo
above the pigeons.

IT'LL BE OKAY, AND YOU WILL BE TOO.

DR. JEREMY GOLDBERG

I am stronger than weakness, brighter than darkness, and braver than cowardice. I am stronger than weakness, brighter than darkness, and braver than cowardice. I am stronger than weakness, brighter than darkness, and braver than cowardice. I am stronger than weakness, brighter than darkness, and braver than cowardice. I am stronger than weakness, brighter than darkness, and braver than cowardice. I am stronger than weakness, brighter than darkness, and braver than cowardice. I am stronger than weakness, brighter than darkness, and braver than cowardice. I am stronger than weakness, brighter than darkness, and braver than cowardice. I am stronger than weakness, brighter than darkness, and braver than cowardice. I am stronger than weakness, brighter than darkness, and braver than cowardice. I am stronger than weakness, brighter than darkness, and braver than cowardice. I am stronger than weakness, brighter than darkness, and braver than cowardice. I am stronger than weakness, brighter than darkness, and braver than cowardice. I am stronger than weakness, brighter than darkness, and braver than cowardice. I am stronger than weakness, brighter than darkness, and braver than cowardice.

IT'LL BE OKAY, AND YOU WILL BE TOO.
DR. JEREMY GOLDBERG

DO YOU REMEMBER

…that time I gave up
the vicious battle
and I raised my white flag?

…the night I accepted
the sorrowful truth
that life had nothing more to offer?

…the day I conceded
the lonely epiphany
that the struggle wasn't worth the fight?

Me, neither.

IT'LL BE OKAY, AND YOU WILL BE TOO.
DR. JEREMY GOLDBERG

Yesterday,
I thought about how
there has to be more
to life than this.

Today,
I'm going to go out
and find it.

IT'LL BE OKAY, AND YOU WILL BE TOO.
DR. JEREMY GOLDBERG

A funny thing happens to the stories we tell ourselves—
we believe them, and then we become them.
We hold our fibs beneath our ribs,
we hide our lies behind our eyes,
and we slowly, stubbornly
turn ourselves into the thoughts
we feed our hearts.

IT'LL BE OKAY, AND YOU WILL BE TOO.

DR. JEREMY GOLDBERG

Inconsolable is a short step from unstoppable. Keep going.

IT'LL BE OKAY, AND YOU WILL BE TOO.
DR. JEREMY GOLDBERG

There once was a man,
a very old man,
who sat on his deathbed
with his head in his hands.

He was all alone,
cold, still, and ready,
when he quietly wrote,
"My name is Nobody."

With his last gasping breath,
he softly scribbled and sighed,
"I regret being myself,"
and then Nobody died.

For those words of his,
they remember him fondly,
but they caution their kids,
"Don't be a Nobody."

IT'LL BE OKAY, AND YOU WILL BE TOO.
DR. JEREMY GOLDBERG

Be present and love your fucking self.
Polish your fucking Zen.
Cleanse your fucking chakras.
Spit-shine your fucking soul and leave your fucking fears at home.
Combine sass with some spirit and enlighten the fuck up.
Get fucking bendy,
downward-fucking-dog yourself,
and let your fucking aura glow.
Believe in fucking karma
and chant some fucking mantras.
Get your fucking om on and radiate some fucking peace.
Today is a good day to manifest the shit
out of some fucking abundance.
Fucking namaste.

IT'LL BE OKAY, AND YOU WILL BE TOO.
DR. JEREMY GOLDBERG

You know when you were little
and your parents tried to get you to eat your vegetables
but they tasted bad
and you didn't want to eat them
and you fought and cried
and screamed and moaned
and got super upset about it,
but then you grew up
and things changed
and years later you once ordered a salad for dinner
and you sometimes steamed some broccoli
and then one day you saw
the things you used to hate,
the bad things that used to taste
so bad were actually good for you
and helped you grow stronger
and bigger and better?
That's what heartache is like.
Heartache is Brussels sprouts.

IT'LL BE OKAY, AND YOU WILL BE TOO.
DR. JEREMY GOLDBERG

In pitch-black nights,
turbulent times,
or when the storms rage,
the only lights I find
are the stars I see
when I close my eyes,
and I know now
what I've suspected for years,
that I can be lost and still
know the way,
that my constellations are enough
and that I can follow them home
because I am already there.

IT'LL BE OKAY, AND YOU WILL BE TOO.
DR. JEREMY GOLDBERG

Sometimes I think about baby birds,
those fuzzy little unborn bastards
just chilling out all calm and quiet inside their shells,
feeling warm and peaceful and perfect,
not a care in the world or a thought in their heads,
and then I imagine the terror and anxiety they must feel as they give in to a
sudden urge to smash their face against the walls that contain them.
No longer content to bear the dark, they fight furious and fast,
violently striking and shattering their shells,
bursting holes in reality until, eventually, light shines in,
a light they never knew existed
but one that brightens their life
and illuminates the truth that walls are built for destroying
and boundaries are nothing but arbitrary encouragements
to trespass on possibilities.
These baby birds clumsily climb out
into a new world with a new vision,
a place they can stretch their wings for the first time
and I sometimes stop and smile and wonder
if they realize what's next,
if they know they will soar over mountains
and fly across sunsets,
if they ever look back and realize they had to crack
before they hatched and hatch before they flew,
but I mostly stop and smile and wonder
about how we do, too.

IT'LL BE OKAY, AND YOU WILL BE TOO.

DR. JEREMY GOLDBERG

Give the space
in your heart
a place
in your life.

IT'LL BE OKAY, AND YOU WILL BE TOO.
DR. JEREMY GOLDBERG

Imagine a box.
Imagine a glass box.
Imagine a big glass box in a big dark room
and imagine you fill it with heart, with soul, with love.
Imagine all of it is filled with all of you,
everything you were and are,
and imagine it filled to the brim,
but imagine it doesn't feel heavy,
it feels light, pure.
Imagine one day the big glass box drops,
smashes and shatters, everything breaks,
all of it all over the place,
pieces of you everywhere.
That's what heartbreak feels like,
orphaned limbs and hollow bones,
stuck.
Now imagine a future,
a later, a soon to come, and a nearly there.
Imagine an unexpected light
from a nook you never noticed,
and imagine it shines on the shards just right
and suddenly the big dark room roars with light,
rainbow reflections, colorful escape.
That's what love feels like.
Love turns our prisons
into prisms.

IT'LL BE OKAY, AND YOU WILL BE TOO.

DR. JEREMY GOLDBERG

The true monsters
aren't the gigantic beasts hiding
silently under the bed
or cowering in the caverns
of your closet.
They aren't bred under bridges
or nurtured in nightmares.
The real monsters are the tiny
daily thoughts you let slip away
unnoticed or unchallenged.
The "what ifs" and the "I can'ts,"
the "I'm not good enoughs"
and "I'm not ready yets."
These are the real monsters to fear.
Drag those bastards out into the light
and show them who's in charge.

IT'LL BE OKAY, AND YOU WILL BE TOO.
DR. JEREMY GOLDBERG

There are no missing pieces
and the hardest lesson learned
is that you already are
the whole damn puzzle.
Just like the real ones,
if you want to complete the picture,
the advice is the same:
Start with the edges
and work your way in.

IT'LL BE OKAY, AND YOU WILL BE TOO.
DR. JEREMY GOLDBERG

Your big heart of gold
deserves more than camouflage.
Let that fucker shine.

IT'LL BE OKAY, AND YOU WILL BE TOO.
DR. JEREMY GOLDBERG

We worship deities and royalty,
divine guides and birthright,
and we fawn over flawlessness,
but no queen was ever pristine
and even gods have haters,
especially gods have haters.
The more we chase perfection,
the less we enjoy and the more we fail,
until we learn the hard way
that every king of consequence
was once a crooked-crowned prince,
and every angel above has a halo askew.

IT'LL BE OKAY, AND YOU WILL BE TOO.
DR. JEREMY GOLDBERG

Those who know me
don't bet against me,
and those who bet against me
don't know me.

IT'LL BE OKAY, AND YOU WILL BE TOO.
DR. JEREMY GOLDBERG

Look closely.
Look harder.
Search the surprise in your eyes,
and when you see the one you need,
right there,
right in front of you,
you'll learn at last,
every mirror hides a hero.

IT'LL BE OKAY, AND YOU WILL BE TOO.
DR. JEREMY GOLDBERG

I know that getting better is hard,
that forgiveness is a stubborn trick,
and that progress is a slow struggle,
but don't you quit.
Don't you ever quit on yourself.
Don't you ever give up.
Don't you ever neglect to remember that deep down,
buried in camouflage and face paint,
there lies a hopeful spark in your heart
that is the most important thing you will ever own.
Choose to believe in that tiny light in the darkness.
Choose to commit to courage.
Choose to challenge everything you see, feel, and believe,
and choose to change it all if nothing is working for you.
Choose to dream big and choose to start small,
one day at a time, one hour to believe,
one minute to manifest something different, new, exciting,
because if you can change your mind, you can change the world.

IT'LL BE OKAY, AND YOU WILL BE TOO.
DR. JEREMY GOLDBERG

YOU'RE AT THE END OF

— *Your Rope* —

and that's **FINE**

TIE IT TO SOMETHING AND

Climb

IT'LL BE OKAY, AND YOU WILL BE TOO.

DR. JEREMY GOLDBERG

May the hope in your heart
rip your darkness apart.

IT'LL BE OKAY, AND YOU WILL BE TOO.
DR. JEREMY GOLDBERG

I felt like nothing mattered,
nothing would ever work out,
nothing would ever be good
or right or fun again,
and I tricked myself into believing
that I didn't deserve love,
that I couldn't find joy,
that I would never be whole again
because I wasn't good enough
or strong enough
or smart enough,
but if we work hard
and keep going,
life has a funny way of proving us wrong.
So work hard and keep going, my friend,
because it's worth it
and you are, too.
You are worth the fight.

IT'LL BE OKAY, AND YOU WILL BE TOO.
DR. JEREMY GOLDBERG

YOU ARE *Worth* FIGHTING *for* *to* THE *Death* WITH A *Butter Knife*

IT'LL BE OKAY, AND YOU WILL BE TOO.
DR. JEREMY GOLDBERG

Some trees are always green,
lush with leaves, abundant and healthy.
That is how they are made.
That is what they are.
They thrive despite the season.
It is okay if you are not this tree.
Not all trees are always green.
Other trees, in some seasons, are leafless,
bare, seemingly structured of nothing
but sticks and brittle hope,
mistaken for dead, they stand proud.
Have you ever met this tree?
Have you ever been this tree?
It is okay to shed your leaves,
to seem lifeless to those who know
no better than to believe just what they see.
They know not your resilience, your strength,
nor the droughts you overcame.
They know not the way you waver
amidst strong winds yet still stand,
big and bold,
nothing to hide behind.
They know not the courage it takes
to bravely battle on each day.
Focus not on the leaves, but on the tree.
The tree still stands.

IT'LL BE OKAY, AND YOU WILL BE TOO.

DR. JEREMY GOLDBERG

Create the days you need
to feed the fires that keep
your dreams alight.

IT'LL BE OKAY, AND YOU WILL BE TOO.
DR. JEREMY GOLDBERG

There are no early stages or final phases.
There is simply a moment,
a revelation,
a turning point of no return
where we must decide to start
seeking and doing and trying,
and then,
every day,
again and again,
another decision to keep going and loving and learning,
and somewhere in that process is life and growth and warmth,
and everything good and pure and true,
but most importantly,
somewhere in that process is you.

IT'LL BE OKAY, AND YOU WILL BE TOO.
DR. JEREMY GOLDBERG

The darkest night
is no match
for the
dimmest light.

IT'LL BE OKAY, AND YOU WILL BE TOO.
DR. JEREMY GOLDBERG

Stop for a moment and breathe.
Stop for a minute and think.
Now, start again.
Start prioritizing fun.
Start glamorizing freedom.
Start searching for adventure, wonder, and awe,
and start dreaming while you're still awake.
Start making memories instead of making money,
and start making progress, not excuses.
Start fulfilling potential.
Start praising the present.
Start thinking about the now,
and start wondering about what's possible.
Start to relax.
Start to unwind.
Start attending moments, not meetings.
Start elevating your spirit, not your pay grade.
Start defining earnings in terms of time well spent,
not dollars and cents.
Start feeling free.
Start living boldly.
Start to breathe again, and start taking your own breath away.
Start sharing your heart and soul and passion with others,
and start now, today, before it's too late.
The world needs you to begin again.

IT'LL BE OKAY, AND YOU WILL BE TOO.
DR. JEREMY GOLDBERG

The world is better
because you're in it.
Don't forget that shit.

IT'LL BE OKAY, AND YOU WILL BE TOO.
DR. JEREMY GOLDBERG

It's about belief.
It's about choice.
It's about choosing,
every sunrise and sunset,
to hold tight
to the things you know you need.

It's about determination,
and it's about diligence.
It's about needing,
each day and each night,
to fiercely fight
for the faith you think you want.

It's about heart.
It's about soul.
It's about wanting,
for us and for them,
to surrender
to the dream you feel you love.

IT'LL BE OKAY, AND YOU WILL BE TOO.
DR. JEREMY GOLDBERG

IT'LL BE OKAY, AND YOU WILL BE TOO.
DR. JEREMY GOLDBERG

Those stars up there shining bright,
some of them are so far away that it takes
hundreds of years
for their light to reach our eyes,
hundreds of years
for their shine to travel
through the vast, dark nothingness of the universe
before we look up and notice their glow,
and so when you ask me why I keep going,
when you ask me why I keep trying
when nothing seems to work
and no one seems to mind,
when you ask me why I even bother anymore,
my answer is this:

"I do it for them.
Stars are my role models.
If they can, I can,
and what better thing to aspire to be
than a humble little light in a big dark world?"

IT'LL BE OKAY, AND YOU WILL BE TOO.
DR. JEREMY GOLDBERG

Go make a fucking
difference in the world.

IT'LL BE OKAY, AND YOU WILL BE TOO.
DR. JEREMY GOLDBERG

Above all else,
through the pouring rainstorms of your soul
and down across the frozen wastelands of apathy and evil
that you may witness,
never stop celebrating.

In time,
you will learn that every emotion is a gift,
that hardship is a younger, dirtier version of wisdom,
and that we are all,
each of us,
miracles in a constant state of grace.

IT'LL BE OKAY, AND YOU WILL BE TOO.

DR. JEREMY GOLDBERG

Today is a good fucking day
to have a fucking good day.

IT'LL BE OKAY, AND YOU WILL BE TOO.
DR. JEREMY GOLDBERG

I'm made of mountains inside,
with some peaks too high for me to climb.
I look inward and up,
but I can't see the top,
and if I can't see the top, how can I rise above?
I choose to walk on instead of just stop.
I choose to keep going when life feels too tough.
I've got stems and leaves in my mind
I've trained over time to strive for the light
despite all the darkness I feel inside,
and while growth, by design,
is a patient process,
a painful project that takes time,
I'm on a perpetual quest to collect silver linings.

IT'LL BE OKAY, AND YOU WILL BE TOO.
DR. JEREMY GOLDBERG

Life is far too serious
to take seriously,
and sometimes the bravest
thing you can do
is laugh.

IT'LL BE OKAY, AND YOU WILL BE TOO.
DR. JEREMY GOLDBERG

Have you ever swum to the bottom of a pool,
and you get down there and you're tired
and your lungs are burning for a breath,
and you're really deep
and you plant your feet
where you can sink no lower,
and you stop and you pause
and you squat and push off,
surge up,
lungs ready to explode,
suffocating,
convinced you'll need gills to live, and then
just below the surface,
just beneath the light,
just when you can hold on no longer,
you break through,
open your eyes,
smile,
and you breathe a great big breath and you feel okay
because you made it back safe?
That's how to deal with hitting rock bottom.
Take a moment to feel it,
accept it,
and then push it away and chase the light
until you can breathe again.
Fighting for light is how we stay alive.

IT'LL BE OKAY, AND YOU WILL BE TOO.
DR. JEREMY GOLDBERG

Punch
YOUR FEARS
IN THE
Face

IT'LL BE OKAY, AND YOU WILL BE TOO.
DR. JEREMY GOLDBERG

Do you want to have a good life?
Turn your good intentions into good thoughts,
and your good thoughts into good actions.
Make bad things good,
good things very good,
and very good things oh-so-fucking good.
Be a good person
who fights for the greater good,
says good goodbyes,
and maintains eye contact
for a good moment too long
when you say goodnight.
Get good sleep,
eat good food,
and do good work.
Be good to yourself,
be good for others,
and make your own good luck.
That's how you have a good life.

IT'LL BE OKAY, AND YOU WILL BE TOO.
DR. JEREMY GOLDBERG

Sharing weakness
is a sign of strength.

IT'LL BE OKAY, AND YOU WILL BE TOO.

DR. JEREMY GOLDBERG

Pay no attention to the doubters,
the naysayers,
the pessimists
always lurking,
haunting,
waiting.
Just do what makes you feel good.
Do what makes you explode inside.
Do what tattoos a smile on your heart.
Do what fills you with hope.
Do what drives you.
Do what you do best,
and do what you love,
and do that for the rest of your life.
You don't have to do it like everyone else,
but you do have to live your best life
and become your best you.
Do it now.
Do it today.

IT'LL BE OKAY, AND YOU WILL BE TOO.

DR. JEREMY GOLDBERG

THE Best Revenge IS A Happy Life

IT'LL BE OKAY, AND YOU WILL BE TOO.

DR. JEREMY GOLDBERG

We are all stardust made of starlight
and every night we look up is a family reunion,
a conscious communion with the unknown
and unbelievable truth that we are all sacred and scared,
suffering and bumbling bundles of beauty
somehow stumbling towards truth and unity,
watching for hope yet tripping on hurt
in a world born from darkness
just like we were.

IT'LL BE OKAY, AND YOU WILL BE TOO.
DR. JEREMY GOLDBERG

The world is filled with lost souls
giving directions to kids
born with compass hearts.

Be brave enough to trust yourself.
Your true north knows the way.

IT'LL BE OKAY, AND YOU WILL BE TOO.
DR. JEREMY GOLDBERG

Strike the
match that
sets your soul
on fire.

IT'LL BE OKAY, AND YOU WILL BE TOO.
DR. JEREMY GOLDBERG

Let it bleed.
Let it heal.
Leave it be.

IT'LL BE OKAY, AND YOU WILL BE TOO.

DR. JEREMY GOLDBERG

Those of us not in prisons build our own.
We use culture as mortar,
peer pressure as bricks,
and we seal ourselves
inside this nonsensical fortress,
a fallacy of false feelings
forced upon us by socially approved
and accepted ideas of what we should do,
whom we should be,
how we should act,
and I'm tired of it.
From now on,
I'm bending these bars
and I'm setting myself free.

IT'LL BE OKAY, AND YOU WILL BE TOO.
DR. JEREMY GOLDBERG

Lakes can freeze,
but life remains underneath.
Hearts, too.

IT'LL BE OKAY, AND YOU WILL BE TOO.
DR. JEREMY GOLDBERG

I don't mind the dust,
I admire the view and
steep steps grow easy
the more you do,
so fight and push
and dream and go
wander routes
not traveled most,
through biting wind
and sleet and snow
embrace pitfalls
and hug potholes
for one day soon
I vow you'll learn
that open roads
carve open souls
and sometimes hope
can feel like home.

IT'LL BE OKAY, AND YOU WILL BE TOO.
DR. JEREMY GOLDBERG

Shining armor isn't something you wear,
it's something you are.
Yes, be the knight that saves the day,
but always remember,
it's not how you look that matters,
it's how you think,
it's how you feel,
it's who you are.
It's how comfortable you are in your own skin,
and it's the things you stand up to defend.
The real shining armor is how kind your heart is,
and the reality is that anyone
who doesn't appreciate a kind heart
isn't being tough,
they're being hard,
and being hard is hard work.

IT'LL BE OKAY, AND YOU WILL BE TOO.
DR. JEREMY GOLDBERG

Live a life THAT WOULD Make YOU Jealous

IT'LL BE OKAY, AND YOU WILL BE TOO.
DR. JEREMY GOLDBERG

I am a fish,
and life is the sea.
Try all it likes,
it'll never drown me.

IT'LL BE OKAY, AND YOU WILL BE TOO.
DR. JEREMY GOLDBERG

I own so many scars
that I pile them up like pillows.
I rest comfortably
(on layer upon layer of lessons learned),
and I hurt easily
(due to sensitive thoughts from a sensitive heart),
but I heal quickly
(because of a brain filled with bandages),
and I promise you,
I vow to you,
I guarantee,
you won't get the best of me,
because I save that bit for me.

IT'LL BE OKAY, AND YOU WILL BE TOO.
DR. JEREMY GOLDBERG

Our lives are slow miracles.
We are the love in our scars
and the fight in our hearts.
Yours still beats
and though you have been beaten,
you will not be beat.

IT'LL BE OKAY, AND YOU WILL BE TOO.
DR. JEREMY GOLDBERG

Trust the spark that
starts the flame that
fuels the fire that
gives the heat that
warms your heart and
frees your mind.
Let that spark blind your eyes.
Let that spark change your life.

IT'LL BE OKAY, AND YOU WILL BE TOO.
DR. JEREMY GOLDBERG

Home is where the heart beats.

IT'LL BE OKAY, AND YOU WILL BE TOO.
DR. JEREMY GOLDBERG

You are art and
you deserve a life
worth framing and hanging
in a gallery somewhere
people stare lovingly
at everything you are.

IT'LL BE OKAY, AND YOU WILL BE TOO.

DR. JEREMY GOLDBERG

Every day I focus on myself
and who I want to be,
the life I long to live,
and the world I need to see.
I'm getting there.
I really am.
Every day, I'm a step closer and a bit better,
one more smile and one less frown,
another fall forward to move me along.
I'm on my way,
and although I hurt sometimes
and it stings when I bleed,
my defeats will not defeat me.

IT'LL BE OKAY, AND YOU WILL BE TOO.
DR. JEREMY GOLDBERG

I don't know how it ends,
and I have no clue how it began.
I don't know your wars and wonders,
the memories that flood your mind and drown your soul.
I don't know whom you long to become,
why or where you want to go.
I don't know your struggles and strife,
the things that haunt your mind and heart,
and I don't know who you are or why you fight,
or for what.
But I do know that gracefully accepting defeat is a victory in itself,
that surrendering is a way of continuing,
that control is a square peg in the round hole of life
and that sometimes you just have to let go, fall inside,
and release yourself to acceptance in order to grow.

IT'LL BE OKAY, AND YOU WILL BE TOO.
DR. JEREMY GOLDBERG

These napalm nights
will pass,
and this cold sunlight
will warm,
but we must not fear
the frostbite
if we ever hope to thaw.

IT'LL BE OKAY, AND YOU WILL BE TOO.
DR. JEREMY GOLDBERG

Climb the mountains of your mind and
scream smiles from the summit.
Note: Shout loud.

Dive deep into the dark caverns in your heart
and salvage the spoils worth sharing.
Hint: It's all worth sharing.

Plunge fiercely into the fear-filled forests
that overgrow your hopes and dreams.
Reminder: Don't forget your chainsaw.

IT'LL BE OKAY, AND YOU WILL BE TOO.
DR. JEREMY GOLDBERG

Scared to spread your wings?
Even birds fly in grey skies.
Soar, motherfucker!

IT'LL BE OKAY, AND YOU WILL BE TOO.

DR. JEREMY GOLDBERG

LIFE LESSONS FROM A SUNSET

Charge straight into the dull and dark unknown,
even if it means changing the way everything looks around you,
even if people stop and stare and point at you,
even if people walk past and silently ignore you,
don't think twice about you,
even if they don't appreciate your light
or the life and warmth you provide,
even if you don't know what tomorrow brings,
even if you fade to black
and can't ever go back to how it used to be,
charge straight into the dull and dark unknown.
That's where the light grows.

IT'LL BE OKAY, AND YOU WILL BE TOO.
DR. JEREMY GOLDBERG

Courage is knowing it might hurt and doing it anyway. Stupidity is the same. And that's why life is hard.

IT'LL BE OKAY, AND YOU WILL BE TOO.
DR. JEREMY GOLDBERG

Do butterflies flop around
reminiscing about the cramped cocoon
from which they escaped?
Of course not.
They're too busy being beautiful
and smelling flowers
and flying places
and doing whatever awesome shit it is
that butterflies do.
You, too, escaped from darkness
and there's no need to thrust yourself
into that dusty little cell ever again.
Stop crying and start flying.

IT'LL BE OKAY, AND YOU WILL BE TOO.
DR. JEREMY GOLDBERG

Sometimes my heart is poverty-stricken
and my soul is on welfare,
and some days
every breath is a battle
and everywhere
is a war,
and
some moments
I feel like raising
a white flag
at my pain
and fear
and hurt,
but I slowly,
stubbornly
raise my middle finger instead.

IT'LL BE OKAY, AND YOU WILL BE TOO.
DR. JEREMY GOLDBERG

Stand outside,
and stare at the stars.
Pretend you're somewhere else,
and then realize that you are.

IT'LL BE OKAY, AND YOU WILL BE TOO.
DR. JEREMY GOLDBERG

I apologize,
but I cannot hear your criticisms,
feel your scorn,
or process your insults,
much less take the time
to appropriately respond
because,
you see,
I have simply been
too busy kicking ass to care.

IT'LL BE OKAY, AND YOU WILL BE TOO.
DR. JEREMY GOLDBERG

We don't take action
because we are brave.

We are brave
because we take action.

IT'LL BE OKAY, AND YOU WILL BE TOO.
DR. JEREMY GOLDBERG

Shine so bright your heart gets a tan.

IT'LL BE OKAY, AND YOU WILL BE TOO.
DR. JEREMY GOLDBERG

Sometimes when you feel like you're
getting kicked while you are down,
it's actually life saving you from getting back up too soon,
and maybe getting bit by a big, scary raccoon
or hitting your head on a helicopter.
Just because you have to stay down a little longer
doesn't mean you won't get back up.
Maybe this pause is preventing more pain
or teaching you to plant your feet before you start again.
Maybe for Halloween you should dress up as a seed,
and maybe the best trick and sweetest treat
is to just let go and breathe.

IT'LL BE OKAY, AND YOU WILL BE TOO.
DR. JEREMY GOLDBERG

I'm just trying to write beauty
over all of the ugly typos
we live through
each day.

IT'LL BE OKAY, AND YOU WILL BE TOO.
DR. JEREMY GOLDBERG

Remind me not all aches are bad,
that black nights still shine light
and even in rainstorms,
or when hail comes,
and the sky is filled
with emptiness we run from,
the sun is always out somewhere.
Remind me I am filled with light.

IT'LL BE OKAY, AND YOU WILL BE TOO.
DR. JEREMY GOLDBERG

I woke up this morning
and realized that if I can wake up
I can get up and if I can get up
I can get going and if I can get going
I can do something and if I can do something
I can do anything and if I can do anything
I can change something and if I can change something
I can change anything and if I can change anything
I can be happy and if I can be happy then
that's a pretty damn good day,
thank you very much.

IT'LL BE OKAY, AND YOU WILL BE TOO.
DR. JEREMY GOLDBERG

May your day,
your year,
your life,
be filled with more "Fuck yes!"
and less "Fuck this!"

IT'LL BE OKAY, AND YOU WILL BE TOO.
DR. JEREMY GOLDBERG

LIFE LESSONS FROM A STRAWBERRY

Give yourself time,
but sweeten as the days go by,
and hide your vulnerable parts outside,
where everyone you see can see them.
Show the world your true colors,
but be unafraid to change your shades.
When it's time to let go, release.
Let yourself get carried away,
and have faith life will take you to a better place.

IT'LL BE OKAY, AND YOU WILL BE TOO.

DR. JEREMY GOLDBERG

We don't cry; we sing,
and like every average bird in any given tree,
and the outbursts and hurts that echo from its beak,
each shriek a simple song with a tender melody,
we sing proud and we learn how
our lives can scream beauty.

IT'LL BE OKAY, AND YOU WILL BE TOO.
DR. JEREMY GOLDBERG

When you stop to smell the roses,
appreciate their thorns.
Notice their flaws
do not define them.
These are not thorn bushes.
They are roses.
So are we.
Bloom.

IT'LL BE OKAY, AND YOU WILL BE TOO.

DR. JEREMY GOLDBERG

I was daydreaming about how shooting stars work,
why their light pierces dark when their flame scalds the sky,
how they come and go as they please,
where they start and when they end,
and I looked down at this creature sitting next to me,
I looked at its colors and looked at its wings,
and I thought about how it used to be
a wandering worm crawling though dirt and mud
looking for a dark place to hide,
and I thought about how this beautiful thing
is the result of a complete transformation,
how quickly things can change,
how it went from walking to flying,
ugly to stunning,
small to big,
and what else do you need to know about life
except that shooting stars roam free and butterflies exist?

IT'LL BE OKAY, AND YOU WILL BE TOO.

DR. JEREMY GOLDBERG

The more I accept,
the luckier I am.
The luckier I am,
the happier I become.
The happier I become,
the stronger I feel.
The stronger I feel,
the more I accept.

IT'LL BE OKAY, AND YOU WILL BE TOO.
DR. JEREMY GOLDBERG

I'll get knocked down,
but I can get up quickly,
and yes,
I'll get destroyed but I can rebuild swiftly,
and when you see me flailing in rough seas
coughing up lungfuls of dark waves
and I'm thinking I'm sinking
because my arms are numb
and I can't feel my legs,
please go ahead and say,
with a hushed assurance
and a knowing grin,
"You'll drown slower if your chin's up, friend."

IT'LL BE OKAY, AND YOU WILL BE TOO.
DR. JEREMY GOLDBERG

Can you do better?
You deserve to do better.
Can you feel better?
You deserve to feel better.
Can you be better?
You deserve to be better.

IT'LL BE OKAY, AND YOU WILL BE TOO.
DR. JEREMY GOLDBERG

KICK TOMORROW IN THE *Teeth*

IT'LL BE OKAY, AND YOU WILL BE TOO.
DR. JEREMY GOLDBERG

Dreams don't come true.
They become true,
and if that becoming
seems to be taking forever,
that's okay.
That's normal.
That's necessary.
Be patient and be brave,
but above all,
believe.

IT'LL BE OKAY, AND YOU WILL BE TOO.
DR. JEREMY GOLDBERG

I'm not perfect, and I don't pretend to be.
I'm a flawed work in progress
trying to make a difference in this world
by making a difference in myself,
and it's a battle, and I struggle and stumble,
but each staggering step forward reminds me
I have what it takes,
and despite my falls and failures,
I am unafraid of great mistakes.

IT'LL BE OKAY, AND YOU WILL BE TOO.
DR. JEREMY GOLDBERG

I welcome rough seas,
don't mind dark clouds.
Storms or swells don't faze me.
I trust the lighthouse in my chest
and know my light won't leave me.

IT'LL BE OKAY, AND YOU WILL BE TOO.
DR. JEREMY GOLDBERG

The haters, the naysayers, and the nonbelievers will never go away, and they will always have their opinions. Don't listen to them. Don't let their fears stand in the way of your dreams. The anteater doesn't give a shit about what the ants think, and neither should you.

IT'LL BE OKAY, AND YOU WILL BE TOO.

DR. JEREMY GOLDBERG

Do you know what they
call too much light?

Pollution.

They call it light pollution.
And do you know what it does?

The lack of darkness dims the stars.

IT'LL BE OKAY, AND YOU WILL BE TOO.
DR. JEREMY GOLDBERG

If you're down on your luck,
make new luck,
make a change,
make a difference,
different thoughts, people, places,
place yourself somewhere kind,
the kind of place you know you need to be,
a place you feel comfortable being alone,
a place you can be you,
because if you're okay with your own company,
lovingly lost in your own happy head and heart,
well,
you'll never be unlucky again.

IT'LL BE OKAY, AND YOU WILL BE TOO.
DR. JEREMY GOLDBERG

REST IN PEACE

Who we used to Be

IT'LL BE OKAY, AND YOU WILL BE TOO.
DR. JEREMY GOLDBERG

Those things you love doing that make you happy?

Fucking do them.

Those people you love seeing that bring you joy?

Fucking see them.

Those words you love thinking but are too scared to mention?

Fucking say them.

IT'LL BE OKAY, AND YOU WILL BE TOO.
DR. JEREMY GOLDBERG

DR. JEREMY GOLDBERG

My mission is to make kindness cool and compassion commonplace. I'm trying to make the world better than it was yesterday. As part of that purpose, I coach clients, write articles, create online courses, host retreats, give talks, and make spoken word poetry videos. I also send out an inspiring and badass email each week, and am active on Facebook and Instagram. For more information about me and how Long Distance Love Bombs began, check out my TEDx talk called "What if kindness was cool?"

WWW.LONGDISTANCELOVEBOMBS.COM

@LONGDISTANCELOVEBOMBS

#LONGDISTANCELOVEBOMBS